Tropical Rain Forests and You

by J. Matteson Claus

Editorial Offices: Glenview, Illinois • Parsippany, New Jersey • New York, New York
Sales Offices: Parsippany, New Jersey • Duluth, Georgia • Glenview, Illinois
Coppell, Texas • Ontario, California • Mesa, Arizona

ISBN: 0-328-13454-6

Welcome to the Rain Forest

Tropical rain forests are among the most **wondrous** places on the planet. Giant trees tower over the forest. Their **dappled** leaves and branches are so thick that little sunlight hits the forest floor. Everywhere you look, this forest is full of life. From the parrot perched on a branch to the snake that **slithered** under a rock, insects, animals, and reptiles of all shapes and sizes roam the forest. Strange flowers fill the air with their **fragrant** scents, and some plants are so bizarre, they don't seem real.

What Exactly *Is* a Tropical Rain Forest?

Tropical rain forests are located around the equator. Temperatures around the equator are very warm. The rain forest stays at a steamy 75°F–80°F all year round.

The *rain* in *rain forest* refers to the fact that they are wet! Very wet! In fact, tropical rain forests can receive between 160 and 300 inches of rain each year. Because the rain forests are always warm and wet, plants grow all year long. The tropical rain forest is home to more plants and trees than any other location in the world!

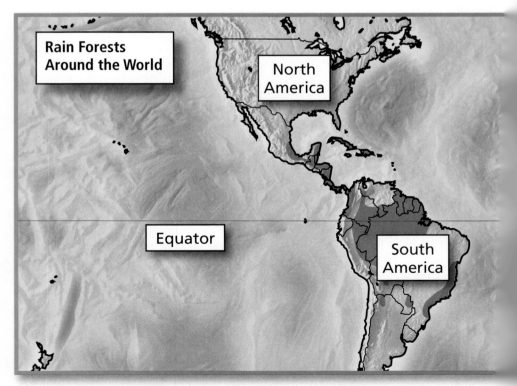

Rain Forests Around the World

North America

South America

Equator

Count on Me, and I'll Count on You

In the rain forest, plants, animals, and people need one another to survive. Almost everything that falls to the forest floor is reused. When plants and animals die, they break down and feed living plants. In turn, those plants give food and shelter to people, animals, and other plants. Water in the rain forest is also reused. It evaporates, forms clouds, and then falls back to Earth as rain.

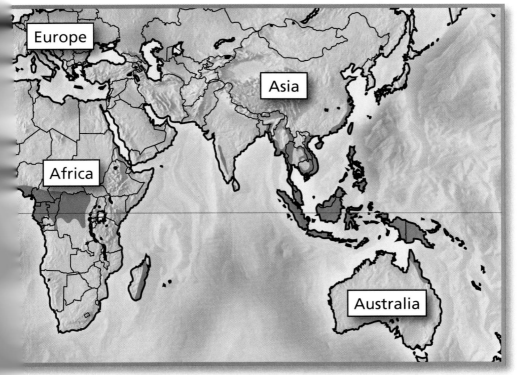

How to Build a Rain Forest

The rain forest is made up of layers of emergent trees, **canopy**, understory, and forest floor.

The *emergent trees* and the *canopy* are the very top layers of the rain forest. Emergent trees are really tall—up to 180 feet high! They're called emergent because they break through, or emerge from, the top layer to reach the sun. This top layer, or canopy, is like a huge, leafy umbrella of tangled treetops. The canopy is so thick that very little sunlight reaches the layers below. Most of the rain forest animals live in the canopy, including birds, tree frogs, and monkeys that **dangle** from the branches.

Peek below the canopy and you'll find the *understory*. Young trees, shrubs, and vines live here, but because there isn't much sunlight, they don't grow very large.

The *forest floor* has even less sunlight than the understory and is quite dark. Fallen leaves and branches rot quickly to provide nutrients for other plants to grow.

Rain Forest Layer Cake

Emergent Trees

Canopy

Understory

Forest Floor

Gifts from the Rain Forest

The rain forests may seem very far away, but you use something from them every day!

For example, do you like chocolate? How about chewing gum? Thank the tropical rain forests! Rain forests are a huge source of food. Fruits such as mangoes and bananas come from the rain forests. So do many nuts, spices, and vegetables.

Many medicines also come from the rain forests, including 25 percent of the ingredients in today's cancer drugs. The plants of the rain forests may hold the cure for many diseases.

One-fifth of the world's fresh water is in the Amazon rain forest. The rain forests actually affect rainfall, which in turn affects climate around the world.

Take a Deep Breath

The rain forests have been referred to as the "lungs" of the planet. That's because the Amazon rain forest provides 20 percent of the world's oxygen. Not only do rain forests provide the air we breathe, but they also reuse carbon dioxide. This helps prevent the rising of Earth's temperature, or global warming.

More than half of the world's species of plants, animals, and insects live in the rain forests. People live in the rain forests too.

9

Green Alert! The Rain Forests Are Disappearing!

Every second, about 1.5 acres of rain forest are lost—that's the size of a football field! If we keep destroying our rain forests, experts predict that the rain forests will be gone within 40 to 50 years. It took millions of years to grow the rain forests. Once they are gone, they can't be replaced.

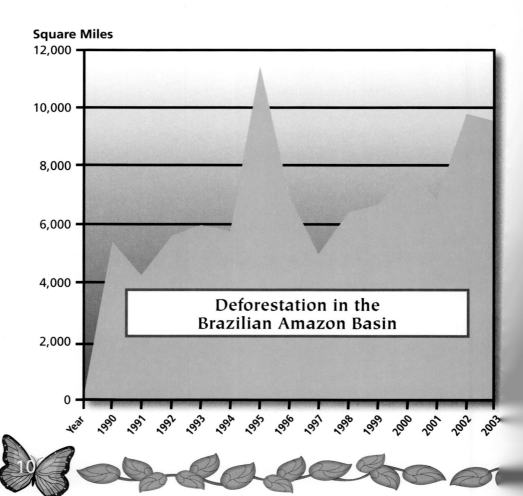

Square Miles

Deforestation in the Brazilian Amazon Basin

The act of burning or cutting down the forests is called deforestation. People who live in the rain forests are careful to take what they need from the forests without causing harm. Outsiders, however, aren't as careful. Settlers and big companies burn trees to clear the land and turn it into farms. Yet only small areas can be farmed at a time. Before long, more of the rain forest has to be burned to create a new farm.

Logging companies cut down trees for timber, or wood. Other companies mine for gold, minerals, and oil. These activities kill plants and wildlife and pollute the water in the process.

The Chain Reaction

The more we cut down and burn our rain forests, the greater the loss of plants, animals, and insects. The loss of one species affects many others. For example, the Euglossine bees, which **pollinate** Brazil's nut

Capybara

trees, can't reproduce without a special type of orchid. These orchids need the bees to carry their **pollen** to other orchids so they, too, can reproduce. If the forest around a Brazil nut tree is cut down, the orchid disappears; then the bees disappear too. The tree doesn't produce nuts, and it vanishes as well!

birdwing butterfly

Could some of the plants being destroyed be a cure for cancer or other diseases? Scientists have only tested 1 percent of rain forest plants. When a rain forest disappears, it's not just the trees that disappear. There's less rain and less oxygen, and there's a danger of the world growing too warm. And when we destroy the rain forest, we take away the homes and the way of life of the native people who live there.

At Home with the Yanomami

The Yanomami are a native people who have called the Amazon home for thousands of years. The little contact they've had with the outside world has been a disaster for them.

Miners have destroyed the Yanomami's homes, brought disease, and poisoned the environment with chemicals. The once-proud Yanomami are dying out.

Losing the entire culture that the Yanomami people brought to the world is tragic. When we lose native people, we lose information about how to live in the forest and how to use all the natural riches without destroying them.

S.O.S: Hope for the Rain Forests

There are many organizations fighting to save the rain forests. By making people aware of the problems related to cutting down rain forests, these groups are helping to save them.

Experts agree that harvesting, rather than destroying, rain forests has more value. We can preserve the rain forests while still collecting their fruits, nuts, and medicinal plants.

You can help too! Recycle! Write to your congresspersons, raise money for organizations that help rain forests, or join an organization. Just knowing how harmful it is to destroy a forest is a big step toward making a difference. In the end, people like you will help a lot in the effort to save the rain forests.

Glossary

canopy *n.* the upper layer, or roof, of the forest made up of the tops of trees.

dangle *v.* to hang loosely.

dappled *adj.* spotted.

fragrant *adj.* having a pleasant odor.

pollen *n.* the fertilizing powder in plants.

pollinate *v.* to bring pollen from one plant to another so it can reproduce.

slithered *v.* glided, slipped, or slid, as a snake does.

wondrous *adj.* extraordinary; causing wonder; to be marveled at.